TRAVELING LIGHT

ALSO BY GERALDINE ZETZEL

Near Enough to Hear the Words (Pudding House Publications, 1998)

With Both Hands (Finishing Line Press, 2004)

Mapping the Sands (Mayapple Press, 2010)

Traveling Light

Poems by

Geraldine Zetzel

Antrim House
Simsbury, Connecticut

Copyright © 2016 by Geraldine Zetzel

Except for short selections reprinted for purposes of
book review, all reproduction rights are reserved.
Requests for permission to replicate should
be addressed to the publisher.

Library of Congress Control Number: 2016946707

ISBN: 978-1-943826-13-1

First Edition, 2016

Printed & bound by United Graphics, LLC

Book design by Rennie McQuilkin

Front cover photograph by Brian Jones

Author photograph by David Buxenbaum

Antrim House
860.217.0023
AntrimHouse@comcast.net
www.AntrimHouseBooks.com
21 Goodrich Road, Simsbury, CT 06070

Acknowledgments

Grateful acknowledgment to the editors of the following publications in which certain poems in this volume first appeared, some in earlier versions:

Ibbetson Street Press: "Repair"
Solstice Literary Magazine: "Survivor"
The Voice (Brookhaven in-house journal): "Worldly Goods"

My thanks to the cadre of dedicated poets in the writing groups that I've been part of in recent years. Their thoughtful reading, energetic critiques and encouragement to venture into new forms and subjects have been a huge inspiration. You know who you are!

I am deeply grateful to all my teachers, especially Suzanne K. Berger, for her inspiring and challenging leadership. She made me read poets I might not have read, and venture to write in ways I wouldn't have dared. Short-term workshops with Fred Marchant, Nadia Colburn, and Sarah Howe also enriched my understanding of the craft of poetry.

Thoughtful readings of the manuscript by Suzanne Berger and Nadia Colburn were immensely valuable in helping bring this collection into a coherent whole. And Rennie McQuilkin's editorial skill and diligence brought the book into finished shape, for which I can hardly thank him enough.

For support and guidance over many years, my deep gratitude to Eric Leibowitz and Narayan Liebenson.

To my dear family and friends: I am so thankful to every one of you for your encouragement throughout this project. You have each helped in your own particular fashion. This book is dedicated to all of you.

Table of Contents

I.

Vienna, June 1922 / 2
The Crime of the Century / 5
Inheritance / 7
Are You Sure? / 8
Lying / 9
A Divorce / 11
Girl with Dogwood / 12
Plane-Spotting / 13
Mirror, Mirror / 14
The Roycemore School for Girls / 15
Impossible / 17
Praise / 19
Waiting / 20
In Iceland / 22
Fathers / 25

II.

Notes from the Far North / 28
Washing Up / 30
Repair / 32
Ode to My Toes / 33
Moonrise, Again / 34
My Brother's Ear / 35
Worldly Goods / 37

III.

Roadside / 40
Insert Rain / 42

Copper Beach / 43
A Fresh Egg / 44
Listen / 46
The Weed-Watcher / 48
A Bunch of Tulips / 49
Turkeys in October / 50
Something Unordinary Persists / 51

IV.

They Are So Close / 54
Pantoum at the Intersection / 55
Survivor / 56
Among Exiles / 59
Graffiti / 61
Schubert at Harbor View / 62
Window / 64

AUTHOR'S NOTE / 66

ABOUT THE AUTHOR / 67

ABOUT THE BOOK / 68

I

VIENNA, JUNE 1922

Summer rain pools on the pavement,
streams off the gaily-tiled roof
of the cathedral. My mother, eighteen,
finds her way alone to the synagogue,
the *Stadttempel*, where she has
never been before.   A spate of rainwater
gurgles down the gutters as she descends
into the basement—to the ritual bath,
the *Mikveh*. *This I am doing for you . . .*
she whispers, holding onto the memory of
his brilliant dark eyes, his musician's hands.
What is he doing this moment,
back in New York, getting ready to bring
his parents here for the wedding?
She tries to imagine, but it's all
too strange, too far and magical.

Inside the building, women in *babushka*s
take charge of her, help her undress,
take away her clothes, instruct her.
They observe how she bathes, making
certain she washes every part of her body—
even her hair, her ears, the soles of her feet.
They scrub her back, then rub her dry
and lead her to the *Mikveh* chamber.
Her towel taken away, she's left alone
at the edge of a square pool. The water is
opaque, with a metallic smell.

I am doing this for love, she tells herself,
as she goes shakily down the steps.
The pool is chilly—her hands rise up
instinctively to protect her breasts.
When the water's shoulder-high,
she dunks herself under three times.

Behind an ornamental screen
the rabbis chant prayers in Hebrew,
at last asking the question:
*Do you desire to become
one with the House of Israel?*
She doesn't understand the words,
but she's learned by heart to
pronounce the answer. Three times
they ask, three times she hears
her own voice say *Ani rozah.*

It's done. She stumbles out of the pool;
the attendants welcome her with towels,
with happy cooing and congratulations.
They help her back into her things.
Who am I now? she wonders
as she stumbles back up the stairs.
*Am I one of Them—that tribe
of odd children mocked in school,
those women wearing ugly wigs,
men in black hats and caftans?*
She could never remember getting home,
only the hot tea laced with rum
her mother brought her. Shivering

as if with fever, she lay in bed
with her alien skin. She never forgot
the greenish water closing over her head,
the way those old women peered
at her nakedness, the guttural voices
questioning her from behind the screen.

THE CRIME OF THE CENTURY

I.

Tucked into bed, I watch the fire-escape rungs
throw shadows on the floor to my cot. Imprisoned.
No escaping the faces staring in—the *baddies*
coming to snatch me. No use calling Fräulein—
"Don't you dare get out of bed!" she says,
"or else . . ." My only comfort that special place
between my thighs. My secret. "Don't touch!"
she warns. But touch I do . . .

> *Four blocks north in Yorkville, the German neighborhood, Bruno Hauptmann builds a crude ladder in his attic, hides it in the bushes near the Lindbergh's country house. Baby Charles was tucked in by his nanny. Almost two, a deep dimple in his chin like his famous flying father. "The child is safe in gut care," the kidnapper writes. "We warn you for making anyding public. Do not talk to police."*

Five years old, what do I know? Only the smell of fear
seeping through the apartment. Fräulein and the cook
whispering in German. Peter and I sip our Ovaltine.
Fräulein knits, listening to Father Coughlin rant
on the radio. She's covered the canary's cage
with a dark cloth to keep him quiet.

> *They call it "The Crime of the Century." Dead, the baby was, all that time. Buried hastily in the woods near the house, with a fractured skull. "The child is mit 2 women," he writes. "They are taking care of him. I must haf the money." Much later, the trial—conviction—execution. Bruno never confesses. No fingerprints, only the ladder. The boot-prints in the mud.*

II.

I outgrow my curls, become a little Swiss girl
with a bob. I speak German at home, French in school.
Peter studies for his Bar Mitzvah—I listen in, add
"Shema Israel" to my nightly prayers. Proud to pray
in so many languages. On Sundays, I walk to Mass
with Fräulein. It's 1937. Hitler, it appears, doesn't like
Jews. I imagine confronting him, just us two,
my black eyes blazing with righteousness
to convince him he's making a terrible mistake.

> *"America First," that's what Lindbergh believes—preferably Anglo-Saxon. "We must limit to a reasonable amount the Jewish influence," he writes, just after Kristallnacht. "Whenever the Jewish percentage of a total population becomes too high, a reaction seems to invariably occur . . ."*

My mother used to meet him at parties.
He was every bit as charming as everyone said—
his nice Midwestern voice, that deep cleft
in his chin, his ice-blue Nordic eyes.

INHERITANCE

Her Papa tended his apple-trees,
hoping to breed the perfect apple;
her Mama knitted an endless scarf,
afraid she might drop a stitch.

One great grandfather is said
to have built a flawless sailboat
that obeyed his every thought.
Another invented a breed of dogs

so smart they could spot
a lie before it was ever spoken.
Was it they who made her wake up
daily in fear of making mistakes?

When she was small, she collected
feathers and white-striped rocks,
hoarding her magic deep
in the secret hollow of an oak.

She was born—like all of us—
yelling, *I want, I want, I want* . . .
Oh what is it you want, they said,
what is it you crave?

The list so long she could not say:
she shut her mouth and looked away.

ARE YOU SURE?

Did they promise to bring you back a present?

Was it the snow globe that time, or the shiny leather box?

Or the book with the marvelous pictures, the kind that were
        covered with sheets of tissue?

Can you remember the other snow globe—
the one that stood on the shelf—in the living-room
        next to the wedding photos?

What was inside it—a woodcutter and a tree
        or a peasant woman with a cow?

Are you sure?

And when you shook it what happened?

Was the little blitz of snowflakes the same every time?

After the snow had settled again, was everything
        just the way it had been before?

No, really—was it exactly the same?

LYING

I used to keep lies the way
some people keep a private zoo
for the joy of their hidden power,
kept them well hidden,
fed them until they were fat
and sleek. Some I trained
to do tricks: big ones that
would come padding to me
when I called them by name,
small ones that learned
to *Roll Over, Beg, Play Dead.*

* * *

A child sits at the dining room table
in front of her plate of cold food.
She will not be excused until
she's chewed and swallowed
every last morsel before her.
Grownups have long ago
left the dining room, gone
to chat over their after-dinner
coffee. She can hear them
laughing, smell their cigarettes.

Eat! If you don't,
we'll have to send you away
to a place where children like you
are fattened like geese—
if they refuse to eat, the nurses
use a tube and a funnel . . .

That's what they said. I thought
it was a lie, but that lie had legs,
that lie had claws. So I chewed
on and on for years, sneaking
bits of gristle to the dog
under the table. Perfecting
my own hidden menagerie.

       *   *   *

What about my own children?
Them I gave the truth, as best I could.
They were free to eat it or not,
to leave it on the plate, slather it
with ketchup. Or feed it to the dog.

       *   *   *

And one day—I can't remember
when—I was ready to let
those sleek old lies go free.
Sometimes they come back
out of the forest and leave
muddy tracks on the porch.
Do I miss them?
No, but once in a while
I set out a dish of milk for them
at night. Or a hunk of salt.

A DIVORCE

Maybe we knew, maybe we didn't.
No slamming doors, no
sounds of weeping.
                One parent
or the other is away, that's all.

Suitcases line the hall.
                Does one of us throw up
every morning before school?
Does one of us cry out at night in terror?

Don't make a scene, that's the rule.

Side by side on the playroom rug
in our bathrobes, we listen to the radio—
The Lone Ranger, Charlie McCarthy,
or was it *Amos and Andy*?
                The dog lies groaning
and farting in his sleep.
Nanny knits under the lamp.
We never asked her:
                she wouldn't have told.

GIRL WITH DOGWOOD

Someday soon she will turn into a tree, like that Greek girl who was pursued by a god. Hounded, yes. They say, *Stop dreaming and put on your socks.* She wonders how it would be to have all those hands and fingers and those eyes made of seeds, and just one set of roots. They say, *Don't chew with your mouth open!* The dogwood blossoms look like a host of open mouths. Host: communion wafer, party-giver, multitude of angels. They say, *Have you done your homework? Written that thank-you note? Wiped out the bathtub?* The pink of the blossoms is like the color of a trout's gills. A trout that's just been fished out of the river. Fish out of water—that's her. They say, *Never talk while you're eating fish—you'll choke on the little bones.* Pink like the inside of the cat's mouth when it yawns. They say, *Cover your mouth when you cough.* The dogwood is holding out her branches. The petals are beginning to whisper their secrets. She can almost hear what they are saying. Soon she will know the language of trees. It's different from human talk. Her body will become a tree-trunk, her arms and legs turn into branches, her feet into roots. Safe, where no one will ever think to look for her.

PLANE-SPOTTING

Summer of 1942, twice a week,
Dad and I climb the Jericho water-tower
to scan the skies for enemy aircraft—
our bit for the War Effort. Happy as two kids
cutting school, we argue about Truth
—or was it God? I'm fifteen, in love
with how ideas run, fly and dive.
But if I begin to win the argument, he gets
huffy, turns pink and barks, *Don't be fresh!*

All we ever sight is the Pan-Am Clipper
looming up over the trees—a practice run
that we duly note down on our shift report.
One time Dad turns to me, suddenly—
I think I'm in love with Mandy Cutler . . .
he blurts. I don't know what to say.
(Was I shocked? Thrilled at being his
confidante? Alarmed that it might
mean another break-up?)
It is never mentioned again.
Summer-time father, six weeks a year.
In other seasons, an erratic flight of blue
airmail letters crossing the Atlantic.

One earlier summer, when I was eight
he used to read aloud to us on the porch
after supper. *The Jungle Book:* voices of
Mowgli, Baloo and Shere Khan
laced with the rumble of thunder moving
over Long Island Sound. The comfort
of sitting there safe, the familiar patter
of lightning bugs and moths beating
soft as rain against the screens.

MIRROR, MIRROR

Mother sits at her
dressing-table arranging

her black hair into two
smooth columns

to frame the symmetry
of her perfect face.

(People say she looks just like
the Duchess of Windsor—

that gaze, that bearing
of the forever loveliest

girl in the room.) Frowning
into the triple mirror

she's fussing with a rogue strand
that won't stay perfectly aligned.

Over her slip she wears
a pale-blue silk cape

to protect her shoulders
from any loose hairs

and to hide from me (all those
long years) the shame

of her scarred chest,
her missing breast.

THE ROYCEMORE SCHOOL FOR GIRLS

Evanston, Illinois

Middy blouse, red bow, pleated skirt: a uniform.
And I'm the new girl, again, the Easterner
doing my best to fit in. The only Jewish kid, but
happy to be in the chorus, singing *Jesus walked
this lonesome valley,* safe among the second sopranos.
Lake Michigan, a block from our house, is wide,
cold as an ocean.
          An awkward household:
Mother, her new husband, who doesn't like
kids, and me, fifteen. No brother now to act as buffer—
Peter's off in the Army. Even our governess
gone at last, might have been an ally
in the face of my step-father's sarcasm,
my mother's helplessness.

No wonder I fall in love with Miss Terry,
the drama coach—her fine profile and jaunty
scarves, the music of her voice.
Each night I write her a letter, to conceal
in our secret "mail box" backstage. And she
leaves me each day a note in return.

Miss T becomes my lifeline. One day, out of the blue,
she calls my mother, asks if I can come to her house
for supper. I remember a dim apartment,
a mousy husband--but mostly the immoderate joy
of being there with Her . . .

And then my mother phones—too early,
to fetch me an hour sooner than planned.
Devastation and rage, the evening ruined . . .
The doorbell rings—furious, weeping,
I go into the bedroom to get my coat.
Miss T follows, takes my face
in her two hands, kisses me on the mouth.

My mother, waiting in the front hall, could not have seen.
But that night, she comes to my room, sits awkwardly
down at the foot of my bed. Then—in what painfully
chosen words—she tries to explain about women
who love other women. She tells me Miss Terry
is one of these, a *Lesbian*—a word I've never
heard before. It sounds like a terrible disease,
a doom, like leprosy—ugly and incurable.

But I can't give Her up—so I decide
it must all be my fault: I am the damaged,
the sick one. For the rest of that year
she remains my Secret Beloved.
And since she is the Princess, I must
be the repulsive one, the toad.

The following year I'm sent back East
to boarding school.

IMPOSSIBLE

I couldn't be—no, I *wasn't*—
just from those few May nights
of besotted love-play
on the Assistant Professor's
lumpy sofa. We didn't really
do it because I really
couldn't—too tight, too uptight,
so how could I possibly (just back
from a summer trip to Italy)
be pregnant?

The rest of my life
(as they say) before me—
two weeks until the start
of my first job—
no way to marry him—
the still-married-but-separated
lover.
It was a no-exit maze,
a haze of terror
but then the respectable
Dr. L, OB/GYN (who was,
it turned out, having an affair with
my therapist) came to the rescue.

Fixed me up, yes he did, admitted me
to the local hospital for a "D. & C,"
all legal and aboveboard
(so to speak).
White room white lights . . .
It all went fine, it's over, he said,

patting my shoulder and
warning me the nurses mustn't find out
the truth—he might lose (this was 1949)
his *privileges.*

Days slide by, cocooned in relief—
life streams through me
like a river of sunlight
from every window
and I lie to the nurses,
the aides, the interns,
my parents when they come
to visit—to myself most:
it was never
a baby . . .

Even when dapper Doctor L.
sitting on the foot of my bed
like a father
explains (what I never
even thought to ask)
*We weren't able to tell if it was
a boy or girl,*
even then it isn't a *baby.*

Not until, on the third day
my breasts
swell hard, my nipples
leak, and I wipe up
their milky tears
and hide the milk-wet washcloth
under the sheets
so the nurse won't see
do I know the truth
and weep.

PRAISE

start wherever you are:
bathing a baby—that gleaming
      that drunken joy
of brand-new skin and soap

a mountainside in Wyoming
cloud-shadows racing
      across its flanks like
a school of dolphins

even the glint of a bit of tinfoil
      in the gutter
even the haunt of a distant
freight-train

these moments when praise
      comes home
as once in Chiapas
the worn stone floor of the church

three zinnias offered up
      in a Coke bottle
one melting candle
just enough light to pray by

WAITING

nights before first birth
          belly-weight
     too heavy
I moon barefoot through
the dark
pacing the heat-
     soaked house
the heft of the Siamese cat
a comfort
      against my shoulder

the city turns in its sleep
distant sirens
rehearse someone's disaster
    what's to come? to be-
come of me? a vessel
am I, hosting what
     will change everything?

that shouldered cat
a practice run, fore-
     runner of
the weeks-later newborn

       her small light body
its weight and startle

me in a trance of fatigue
     her breath a quick

uncertain flutter
into the hollow cup
of my neck

milky moonlight
       seeps in the window
spins undiscovered
galaxies
across the nursery floor

IN ICELAND

1

Stuck at the airport hotel, they
were waiting, like so many others,
for a cloud of volcanic ash to lift.
Nothing to wear but the summer clothes
they'd packed for Italy, nothing
to read but three Penguin mysteries
bought at the Rome airport. An impasse
that resembled their own:
her disappointment, his driving need
for things to happen just as planned.

2

What she remembers is herring for breakfast
every day—and the boredom, palpable as fog.
That strange flat light erasing all shadows,
the sky in endless foreplay with the dark.
Once only, the electric crackle and eerie
greenish flare of the Northern Lights . . .

3

The airline paid for their stay, provided amenities:
bus trips out to the thermal springs, to the national
stud-farm to see the Icelandic ponies. Was it there
the exchange student from Pisa attached herself
to them? Homesick already, she sat with them
in the cafe, asking eagerly about America.
Her schoolbook English, their hesitant Italian.

4

It was in Florence she'd felt it first.
At the Bargello, wasn't it? Not pain,
more like a sort of flutter in her groin.
It came and went. *Probably nothing*, she thought.
Two days later, waking early to that metallic taste
on her tongue, sort of like tin-foil, she knew.
She said nothing to him. Better
to wait until they were home.

5

Years later, in a shoebox, she finds
postcards she sent the children.
How easily we lie, she thinks—
*Today Mom and Daddy went to see
this famous church. It's called
the Duomo.*
In a card from Rekyavik:
*We're having fun in Iceland. See you soon!
We miss you so much.*

6

At the hotel, dinner is served at five.
Stewed lamb with boiled potatoes, mostly.
They try to teach the Italian girl how to play
Hearts. The posters in the lobby—why does
she remember this?—volcanoes and ponies.
Polite good-nights to the others, then up
to their room, white and cool as a cell.
They undress in silence, take turns at the basin,

get into their separate beds, switch off the lamp.
The sky outside the window is ashen, luminous.
By then she knows she's pregnant again.
He had made his position clear a year before:
No more children, two is enough.

7

We went to the thermal springs today,
they were amazing, one postcard says.
It stays with her for years: those little geysers
—life breaking through—bubbling up out of green turf
right next to an ice-field. Those people
who trusted life enough to keep on building
towns on the skirts of volcanoes.

FATHERS

You—in the old snapshot—balance
our firstborn out along the length
of your arm, as if to inspect a rare folio
or an artifact just dug up from deep earth.
Her head's cupped in your palm, her feet
propped in the crook of your arm,
the two of you face to face, amazed
at this tremendous encounter.
These days young fathers tuck a baby
under an arm, like a football, or pack it
clamped between elbow and rib cage
like a package of laundry. The babies
dangle, heads bobbing on stalks,
unsurprised as they sail by, some
wailing, some sucking on a binky.

In Whole Foods the other day,
passing the heaped up display of
pumpkins, a man wore his baby buckled
to his chest like a catcher's shield,
a Starbucks *grande* in one hand,
a phone in the other. *Do we need butter
and what about the sparerib special?*
The child's head lolls, her eyes
glassy, half-closed—she's falling
asleep, floppy as a doll. The skin
of her arms gleams like satin.
Drawn after as if caught up in their wake,
I push my cart as far as the meat counter
just to bask a bit longer in their ease.

HOLD STILL

Gulls in a line on the beach
watch as one of them worries
a crab. Another hunts for scraps,
scavenging boldly among
beach towels.

Golden Lolitas practice cartwheels
while their small brothers in droopy
swim trunks chase each other,
howling with glee, throwing
fistfuls of sand.

Hip-deep in the surf, fathers
stand dunking babies;
under beach umbrellas mothers
anoint the necks of toddlers.
Hold still! they say.

This could be us, fifty years ago.
Look—aren't those our children
charging into the waves? Isn't that kid
with the Frisbee their friend—
what was his name?

At the horizon, as always, a tanker sits,
moving so slowly you can't see it move.

II

NOTES FROM THE FAR NORTH

Here on our ice-floe
we drift in amiable harmony
admiring on winter nights

the pale-green crackling curtains
of the Aurora Borealis.
Beside the whale-oil lanterns

some of us hold hands, others
hunker down hooded, solitary.
By sputtering light we tell

each other the stories
of our previous lives—
our histories keep us warm.

From time to time, of course,
someone slips off the edge
into the black water. It happens.

Then we sew their names into
sealskin boats, float them out
into the waves, chanting the old words.

On clear nights we sometimes can see
the mainland, its fires star-blue
across the sheet ice between us.

From time to time they send us
parcels--used blankets, biscuits,
pemmican wrapped in old newspaper.

In summertime cargo ships
steam past in the distance, busily
steering away southwards.

Do we mind? Of course.
They say we are content,
resigned—don't believe it.

WASHING UP

The dishes, he insists, are his job.
Brought up to use brain, not hands,
now in our late marriage
eager to master new skills—running
the vac, taking out the trash—
doing the dishes becomes
the chore he loves best.
He shoos me out of the kitchen,
never consenting to let things
just soak in the sink until morning.

Nightly, he takes on the grease,
scours the pots with the zeal of a true
believer, *davening* over the suds,
the water scalding hot
as in a surgery scrub-room.
He marshals the cutlery like a troop
of scouts—forks, knives, spoons,
serving-pieces in orderly ranks
into the dishwasher, counters wiped.
And so comes up to bed at last,
his hands smelling of Lemon Joy,
his face rosy, hot as a lover's.

Even in the late bad years, so much
drained, lost from his memory,
he keeps up this blessèd routine.
Slower and slower, the familiar
movements, yet unstoppable.

I try spiriting off the dishes so fast
there'll be nothing left for him to do.
Until I see—why not sooner?—how much
he needs to keep up his husbandry,
to be useful still—at least in this—
and thereafter leave a token plate,
a fork or two, a pot resting in the sink
for the dear work of his shaky hands.

In memory of Lou

REPAIR

When his tea tasted
like toilet paper,
his oatmeal like wet socks—
and when getting out of bed
was like pushing a wheelbarrow
full of rocks up a sandhill,
he thought of all the things
he could no longer do or
couldn't face doing. And
the pain, always the pain . . .

Until the day he remembered
the table lamp he'd meant to fix,
its base a sea-blue vase made by
his mother years back.
Somehow he got himself dressed,
somehow made it to Tru-Value Hardware.
Got the cord, a new socket and plug.

He took the thing apart
on the kitchen table. Tossed
the dusty bulb, frayed wiring
and rusted-out switch
into the trash—they made
a satisfying thud.

At last, setting the lamp down
on his desk, he switched it on—
and the cells everywhere
in his body one by one
began to stir and lighten,
able again to take up
their hidden essential work.

ODE TO MY TOES

after Neruda

You ten good companions
on this long road,
how much I owe you!
Rosy buds you once were,
good little piglets lined up
for their treat . . .
Now all askew, askance,
please keep me toddling,
oh my tootsies—
even though one of you
has to clamber over the next,
even though your porky neighbor
has mislaid its sense of direction
and is pushing
all of you sideways.
Tough as roots, you've
turned turnip, gnarly with work.
Rubbing Arnica into your crevices,
I praise you, valiant travelers!

MOONRISE, AGAIN

Spill of white honey
on the bedroom rug.
Light sliced & checkered
as it filters through
the Venetian blinds.
Dogs near and far
vexed into barking.
Every tree bathed
in mother-of-pearl.

Ah, not to sleep! To stay
awake all night while it lasts!
Not to waste a drop of this
ancient moon-dance.
This old enchantment.
And again the thought—
it might be possible to live
like the moon. Just
coming and going forever,
never having to leave.

MY BROTHER'S EAR

Side by side on the sofa, we peer
at the screen, Peter and I.
We haven't sat so near for years.
Up close, his ear looks large and
noble, like a Pharaoh's. His cheek
glows fresh, rosy as a boy's.

Old now, both of us, we watch
home movies, the fragments of our
fragmented childhood skittering past.
Scenes jump about, now Central Park
now Switzerland. Sailboats glide past
and skiers, birthday parties,
grandparents waving, an ocean liner...
Our dog tirelessly chases
a tennis ball. And here is our mother
—dazzling as a movie star—
hamming it up for the camera.
She's smiling, talking, gesturing...
What is she saying?

The landscape of my brother's ear,
close-up, is like some just-discovered
life-form—a newly found crustacean
or an exotic desert plant.
This same ear that pressed
against my forehead at dancing school
as we practiced the foxtrot.
That bent towards me after lights-out
as we traded information, like spies

trying to figure out the lay of the land.
It's still with me—the sour-sweet flavor
of those shadowy times.

Watching that old life flicker
I feel a rueful pity grow in me
for who we were. That bony boy,
trying over and over to do a cartwheel,
determined to get it right. That skinny
girl—her knock-knees, her fierce scowl—
struggling to keep hold of a puppy.

And there we are, two children dressed up
for some costume party, two awkward
pirates standing side by side in front
of a hotel portal. On holiday in Austria
maybe, or Italy—grinning gamely, our
arms laced tight around each other's waist.

WORLDLY GOODS

They're only *things*—I know, I know:
Impermanent, the Buddha would say.
But tell me what to do
        —right now, I mean—
with this mass of leftovers, these lifetimes
muttering & rustling
        in every cupboard.

This set of open-work ivory linen, for instance
        we got in Florence—place-mats,
        runner, a dozen napkins to match.
Or my parents' wedding silver, complete with
        twelve oyster forks, ten butter knives
        & six egg spoons washed in gold . . .

And here are the cigarette boxes & ashtrays
        we used to put out for parties,
here the leaky beautiful Raku vessels
        from my days as a potter.

Nobody wants our Danish Blue wedding china
or the treasured record collection—
        Casals playing Bach, Burl Ives,
        Dylan Thomas—oh that bardic, drunken voice!—
        The Play of Daniel, Guys and Dolls, Candide . . .

And what to do with movies of birthdays & graduations,
        boxes full of photo negatives, carefully catalogued?
These journals of trips—each day recorded
        with notes, addresses of people we met,

receipts from famous restaurants,
The Dordogne—Sicily—the Fjords of Norway.
Guidebooks—Indonesia & Mexico & Greece?
      And maps, oh those marked & re-folded maps,
his pocket Atlas,
      both our cancelled passports.

And then there's this mountain of books:
      who now will want
Masefield's Collected Works bound in leather,
The Oxford Companion to English Literature (1948)
& all the slim volumes of essays & poetry,
      fly-leaves inscribed with the names
      of old lovers & dead friends?

Ah, tell me, anyone—how do I travel light,
with all these beloved useless things
clinging to my legs like so many children
      babbling their stories?
Are they afraid of the dark?
What shall I tell them,
      how can I comfort them?

III

ROADSIDE

The big male giraffe glides
through the brush,
intent on shepherding
his pod of wives and calves.
The tourist's lens
has caught the flow
of those pacing legs,
steady as oiled pistons.
And the almost comic dignity
of that crowned head.

The sound of the wind
is captured too, and the low
appreciative murmur
of human voices. Missing
only are the smells—
scents of acacia,
thorn-bush and dung,
distant whiff of carrion.

Watching a friend's safari
movies, I think of you and me
and Bea, that time we were
stranded by a flat tire
on a red-dirt road
somewhere near Limuru.
John had flagged down
a passing lorry, gone for help.
You smoked cigarette after
cigarette. Heat shimmered off

the hood of the car. Birds
bounded, whistling
in and out of the trees.

The motor ticked
like some large insect as it cooled.

Then out of nowhere came
a trio of giraffes. They grazed
just beyond the roadside hedge,
peacefully pulling leaves
one at a time from the thorn-trees
with their long clever lilac
tongues. So near we could
smell their heat, hear their
steady chewing. So near
we could see the long
eyelashes framing those
placid luminous eyes.

in memory of Bea and John Whiting

INSERT RAIN

into this poem, to soften its fabric,
to let its colors run
this way and that, like a drift
of clouds unpacking
                after a storm.

Insert rain into a story, to melt
sharp lines, gentle the edges,
let in ambiguity. Make room
for whatever wants
                to happen next.

The way, after Spring rains,
the creek back of the cabin
takes on a low music, the snow-melt
waters foaming ice-green
                over boulders

and the willows stand soaking
up to their knees. And a kingfisher
arrives to feed on the trout.
Now: insert the blue streak
                of his dive.

COPPER BEECH

Like a great fountain above
the city street it towers all summer—
massive trunk grey as a wet seal,

dark mass of limbs and leaves
looming like an August
thunder-head (though one branch

reaches out a long ungainly hand
to passers-by, as if asking to join
the lesser world).

In Spring, while other trees
leaf out in tints of green
and rose and mauve

this giant stands there, noble head
still bare. Each year in May,
I think *This time it must be dead.*

Each year, suddenly flaring
open its dark buds
again, it proves me wrong.

A FRESH EGG

Spooning out the marigold-
yellow yolk, cutting up
the springy white—this treat
needs no salt or pepper
and butter would be
a sacrilege. It tastes
so homely, familiar,
almost holy . . .
          Who was it, I wonder—
that first human being
to dare eat an egg?
I picture some famished
prehistoric mother, foraging
on the wide savannah,
who stumbles on a nest
in the brush, grabs at the bird—
and misses. She finds her hands
coated with golden sap and
sticky, translucent juice,
brings fist to mouth, sniffs,
begins to lick the odd stuff
off her fingers one by one,
savoring that new taste—
and goes home to the cave
to tell the others about her find.

Sated, I sit a while longer
at the breakfast table
picking with my fingernail

at the pliant membrane
that sticks to the shell's inside,
remembering Miss Bellamy—
the Science teacher
I had a crush on in 6\th Grade—
demonstrating *osmosis*.
Holding up the innermost tegument
of a hardboiled egg, she told us,
This is what's called a semi-
permeable membrane.

for Becky Minard

LISTEN

to spring peepers emerged
again in the woods—you can
hear them piping day and night
down in the vernal pool.
Me! Me ! Me! they bleat—
like every living thing.

Spring is all the rage this year
as the long hard winter slowly
gets cleared away. The season
coughs itself into life, an old
flivver's rusty motor
turning over.

Nests are being re-invented
out of winter's scraps,
roadside weeds are primed
to rush up out of every crack
in the pavement.

Listen—I'm just as full of grief
and doubt as you are—what is
this frenzy? And why
should we care? Does any
of this stop all the suffering
even for a moment?

No, but all the same,
I can't help greedily inhaling
the sun, the frog-music,
the blackbird's urgent call
from the swamp.

Sliding open the porch door
I'm like the cat. He bounds out
to crouch on the railing, his ruff all
a-tremble in the sun—such lust,
such yearning...

THE WEED-WATCHER

From first nubbins poking up
out of cracks in the highway,
out of strips of curbside dirt,
fissures in the sidewalk,
I've been watching them
all season. As though to learn
some lesson about survival.

A motley nation of weeds
geysering up like Old Faithful—
the Ragweed's silvery tops
reaching up week after week
to tower tall as a schoolchild
by early September.
The False Bamboo thickens
by the roadside into a jungle
to rocket high in triumph
before it pales to brown,
fades & topples the first cold night.

What is it about this old story?
Maybe that stubborn energy,
the will to surge upwards over
& over, ugly or pretty or plain.
Maybe the music of their names—
Burdock & Bullthistle
Foxtail & Knotweed—
this loveliness against all odds.

A BUNCH OF TULIPS

How their leaves creak,
protesting as I fit them into the vase,
      the flowers holding prim
yet one or two, resisting,
      flop sideways, heads nodding.

Next day they explode
like schoolchildren on a Friday
      rushing out of doors
tossing backpacks
& jackets
      crazy-free, falling
all over themselves,
mouths open
      to drink in joy
& who am I to say
this joy won't last?

TURKEYS IN OCTOBER

Pompous as politicians
they drift across the road,
stopping traffic, haunt
suburban shrubbery,
their bronzed black plumage
ominous, shiny with self-regard.
Above those bulbous bodies
their silly little heads
swivel like radar, scouting.

Conscience some days
arrives like that
in its dark-feathered habit
sidling in on stealthy feet
to inspect your secret garden,
eager to snap up whatever
grubby evidence
you may have dropped.

SOMETHING UNORDINARY PERSISTS

after Charles Wright

The rain-struck dogwood is shedding starfish
        one by one, and the tulips,
pale-poor ghosts of themselves, bow down
           in the cold-hearted wind.
Maple-wings paper the porch floor,
        a failed plantation of seedlings.
The party is over.
None of this is news to the soul, that lurker,
        hunkering down to out-wait
all weathers, knowing that, come evening,
        evensong will always win—
the mockingbird rehearsing his riff in the oak,
the thrush announcing true love
        from the top of the birches.

Is this enough? What of the hungry ghost
that creeps in, requiring more cake, more clowns—
        the one who asks, *Where is the pony?*

Enough is another landscape: snow-melt, lake-shine
        and a river whose greenest music
you've always known by heart.

IV

THEY ARE SO CLOSE

The dead in their cloud of knowing
      seem at times to move near,

their words of praise, or warning, or regret
      rustling like shallow waters.

They crowd around, these May nights,
      close as the trees across the road,

dark shapes facing my sleeping windows
      where some startled bird I never see

lets flower a sudden music at 4 A.M.—
a dawn song before dawn has begun.

PANTOUM AT THE INTERSECTION

Mid-March. Dirty snow and frozen mud.
Geese have arrived to forage the traffic island,
poking their beaks into barren dirt, looking for grass.
The panhandler tramps back and forth in time with the lights.

The geese have arrived to peck at the median strip—
the pickings are scant but they persist.
The panhandler's feet have carved a muddy furrow:
I know his walk, his cardboard sign, his cup.

Pickings are scarce this chilly evening—
I fumble around in my bag for a dollar bill.
The man walks slower, holds out his Starbucks cup,
but the traffic stream is relentless—I have to drive on.

Fumbling to find my money, I've missed my chance—
some kinds of hunger know no season.
The stream of traffic moves on, urgent, relentless.
The light's gone green, the man's turned back on his track.

Some kinds of hunger know no season.
I stuff the bills in the cup-holder for another time.
The light's turned green, the man has wheeled around.
Mid-March—the geese—his freezing, muddy feet.

SURVIVOR

In the Grip of Cold, Afghan Family Buries 8th Child —
News Item, Feb. 8, 2012

I am what's left:
this girl who stands watching
as my father and uncles
              wash my brother's body
for burial. Neighbors have brought us
warm water for the washing: we ourselves
              had nothing left to burn.

Khan's body is a white bundle
on a white sheet; his feet point down
as though he's on tiptoe,
              his mouth a thin line,
like an old man who has made up his mind.

Last night all the paper and straw I'd collected
got used up brewing tea
              to drink with our bread.
Khan was lucky: he could nurse, and find sleep
wrapped in his too-big sweater
              and the yellow blanket
those foreigners gave us.

But then he woke up and cried;
              he struggled all night.
We listened to him cry,
lay sleepless, shivering on the hard ground,
              sharing our blankets.

Mother tried to nurse him but he
turned his head away
so she held him against her body
                      and sang to quiet him.
At last he was quiet.

Cold, you had taken him for yourself,
the way last winter
you took my brother Amir
and the children from other families
                      whose bodies lie out there
in the wasteland behind the camp,
their headstones like fingers of many hands
                      reaching out of darkness.

I am what's left: all of my brothers gone—
                      three of them back in our village
before I knew them—just names now.
Then the twins, Jabir the strong one, and small Sayid—
they died of the Coughing Sickness.
That was before we left the mountains,
trekked many days to this camp outside the City.
                      On the way, Rafik, who used to
carry me on his back, got sick in his belly,
and died by the roadside.

They said here we would be safe from the fighting:
                      we would get clean water,
food, tents, blankets. Sometimes
foreigners come
                      with cooking oil or charcoal
or blankets.

They keep on asking questions: *Where did you come from?*
                         How old are you? How many
                         brothers and sisters do you have?
They put answers down in their notebooks.
Then they go away.

Cold, you have won the war
                         the soldiers can't finish.
I am Ferouza—my name means *turquoise*
like my mother's wedding necklace:
                         the one she sold to the trader
                         for charcoal.
In our village I would be old enough to be betrothed.
I am ready. Cold, soon I will be yours.

Now they are carrying Khan's body
                         out to the back field.
The mullah is starting to chant.
No women are allowed to follow
                         but I am only a shadow.

My father's face is ice, and icicles trail
                         from his beard.
Let him not hear me cough—
his face darkens
when he hears me coughing.

Cold, let him not know
                         that I am to be your bride.

AMONG EXILES

after *The Poet, or Half-Past Three*

Chagall's homage to his friend,
another exile who used to drop by
his studio in Paris at odd hours
for a glass of vodka
and a gossip in Russian.

We stand there
trying to make sense of the image.
The French *tricolor* swirls around
the figure—but Chagall's painted
his friend's head floating upside-down
and bright green—a loose balloon—
drunk with joy at being alive.
Or is it the homesick green of exile?

My stepdaughter's face today
seems all eyes and cheekbones.
Her bald head is swathed
in a silky turban—she's elegant
as a tsarina. I can hardly bear it.

One other woman, I notice,
has her head covered,
despite the August heat.
Tall, rail-thin, she's pushing
a stroller—the baby's asleep,
a blue and white cocoon.
She stands a long time there
in front of that Chagall.

Is she, too, exiled from the country
of ordinary life—her world
turned upside down—trying to master
this difficult new terrain?

GRAFFITI

Not just name-tags scrawled
on a boarded-up window
but these crazy feats—to conquer
towers & buttresses & tilting walls,
to emblazon **SCAZZ** in 2-foot-high letters
to rival **SKARDINO**'s brilliant jigsaw
of black outlined in neon yellow—
skywalkers leaving their marks,
each letter muscular as an acrobat.

Now as the train gains speed
BUCKKE rules along the tracks,
his sign on every overpass & switchbox
into New Jersey, where **OBONTO**
takes over outside Newark.
Then, nearer New York, **TREGG**
appears in purple and gold
on factory wall & storage shed.

Someone has tried in vain
to scrub them off. But they
just go on springing up like
the invasive kudzu and the bittersweet—
beautiful rovers making themselves
at home: **TOPH & KRODITE & SPEXX,**
oh urban heroes, I salute you all—
inventors & night warriors
with your spray-can weaponry,
your elaborate orthography,
your terrible, urgent need to make
some mark on the passing world.

SCHUBERT AT HARBOR VIEW

Praise be to the two young women walking onto the stage,
> for they are lovely and slim as herons in their flowing
> blue skirts.
Praise be to the violinist's Slavic cheekbones and the ice-blue
> eyes of the pianist; they flash fire as she bends to the
> runs of the scherzo.

Praise be to the articulation of the fingers, the opposable
> thumbs, the joints of the wrists;
> their beauty is as the dance of the bees.
The violinist's whole body dances with each stroke of her bow;
> praise be that her body is unable to resist the music.
The pianist's feet caper over the pedals;
> praise be the fifteen bones in the foot.
Give thanks for the brightly lit hall, the comfortable seats,
> for the American flags with their gilt tassels.
Give thanks for the old, who sit in rows to hear the music,
whose hands and bodies and feet remember, who drink in
> the music, who float in the music
> like seabirds on the swell.

Behold: their walkers and wheelchairs are ready, waiting to
> fly up in a cloud, like a host of swallows at evening.
Behold: the hearing-aids and glasses, orthotics, braces and
> canes—they lift up their heads like young colts let out
> to pasture.

Yea, out of nights in the belly of freezing caves,
> out of being born and dying and a need beyond language
> came the two-note flute carved from the bone of
> a mastodon—came music.

Yea, out of a young man on fire, tramping through the slush
 of Vienna to his cold room; from his pen, his ink,
 his lamp, his scraps of cheap used paper,
 this music.
O give thanks for a soul that could imagine such
 a beautiful noise.

WINDOW

You come into a room
      looking for something
and smell leftover coffee.

The window looks back at you
      blank as a newborn's gaze.
What was it you were looking for?

You press your forehead
      against the window-glass.
It's cool, alive with promise.

Dusk gives you back
      a wavering image: your face,
facing into the night. Oh yes,

that's it, that's all: to be alive.

AUTHOR'S NOTE

Some of the apparently autobiographical poems in this volume (e.g., "In Iceland") are fictional.

ABOUT THE AUTHOR

Geraldine Zetzel has been in love with poetry since 5th Grade, when she produced her first sonnet. In addition to her full-length collection, *Mapping the Sands,* she is the author of two chapbooks, *Near Enough to Hear the Words* and *With Both Hands.* Currently, she teaches courses in the Tufts Osher Lifelong Learning Institute, the most recent being focused on African-American poets. A longtime practitioner of Theravada Buddhism, she leads several ongoing meditation groups. Geraldine Zetzel lives in Lexington, MA.

This book has been set in Garamond, a typeface created by Claude Garamond in the first part of the Sixteenth Century. He based his font on types cut by Francesco Griffo for Venetian printer Aldus Manutius in 1495. Garamond created a typeface with an unprecedented degree of balance and elegance, for centuries standing as the pinnacle of beauty and practicality in type-founding. Italics for the Garamond font are based on those cut by Robert Granjon (1513–1589).

To order additional copies of this book
or other Antrim House titles, contact the publisher at

Antrim House
21 Goodrich Rd., Simsbury, CT 06070
860.217.0023, AntrimHouse@comcast.net
or the house website (www.AntrimHouseBooks.com).

•

On the house website
in addition to information on books
you will find sample poems, upcoming events,
and a "seminar room" featuring supplemental biography,
notes, images, poems, reviews, and
writing suggestions.